First World War
and Army of Occupation
War Diary
France, Belgium and Germany

51 DIVISION
Divisional Troops
258 Brigade Royal Field Artillery
1 May 1915 - 22 August 1916

WO95/2854/5

The Naval & Military Press Ltd
www.nmarchive.com
Published in association with The National Archives

Published by

The Naval & Military Press Ltd

Unit 10 Ridgewood Industrial Park,

Uckfield, East Sussex,

TN22 5QE England

Tel: +44 (0) 1825 749494

www.naval-military-press.com

www.nmarchive.com

This diary has been reprinted in facsimile from the original. Any imperfections are inevitably reproduced and the quality may fall short of modern type and cartographic standards.

© **Crown Copyright**
Images reproduced by permission of The National Archives, London, England, 2015.

Contents

Document type	Place/Title	Date From	Date To
Heading	WO95/2854/5 258 Brigade Royal Field Artillery 1915 May-1916 August		
Heading	51st Division 258th (Highland) Bde RFA May 1915-Aug 1916 Bde Broken Up		
Heading	51st Division 1/3 Highland R.F.A. Vol I 1-5-31-7-15		
War Diary	Bedford	01/05/1915	02/05/1915
War Diary	On Active Service	03/05/1915	31/07/1915
Heading	51st Division 1/3rd Highland Bde R.F.A. Vol II From 1 to 31.8.15		
War Diary	On Active Service	01/08/1915	31/08/1915
Heading	51st Division 1/3 Highland Bde R.F.A. Vol III Sept 15		
War Diary	Aveluy	01/09/1915	30/09/1915
Heading	51st Divn 1/3rd Highland Bde R.F.A. Vol IV Oct 15		
War Diary	Aveluy	01/10/1915	30/10/1915
Miscellaneous	Perforated Sheet giving detail of personnel and horses wanting to complete, shown on Army Form B. 213.		
Miscellaneous	Field Return.		
Miscellaneous	For information of the A.G.'s Office at the Base. Officers and men who have become casuals, been transferred or joined since last report.		
Heading	51st Division 1/3rd Highland Bde R.F.A. Nov 1915 Vol V		
War Diary	Aveluy	01/11/1915	30/11/1915
Miscellaneous	Field Return.		
Miscellaneous	Perforated Sheet giving detail of personnel and horses wanting to complete, shown on Army Form B. 213.		
Heading	1/3rd Highland Bde R.F.A. House Dec Vol VI		
War Diary	Aveluy	01/12/1915	31/12/1915
Heading	1/3rd Highd. Bde R.F.A. Jan 1916 Vol VII		
War Diary	Albert	08/01/1916	08/01/1916
War Diary	Albert	01/01/1916	10/01/1916
War Diary	Albert	03/01/1916	03/01/1916
War Diary	Warloy	07/01/1916	07/01/1916
War Diary	T Sauveur	09/01/1916	12/01/1916
War Diary	T Sauveur	11/01/1916	31/01/1916
Miscellaneous	Note Of Ammunition Fired. XV		
War Diary	St Sauveur	01/02/1916	29/02/1916
War Diary	Villers Bocage	01/03/1916	06/03/1916
War Diary	Hem	07/03/1916	08/03/1916
War Diary	Rebreuviette	09/03/1916	29/03/1916
War Diary	Gunposition	30/03/1916	31/03/1916
Heading	1/3 High Bde Rfa Vol X		
Heading	1/3 High Bde		
War Diary	Near Marocul	01/04/1916	30/05/1916
War Diary	Near Anzin	01/06/1916	30/06/1916
Heading	War Diary of 258th Brigade RFA Shown as 257 Bde. 1st July 1916 to 31st July 1916 Volume		
War Diary	On active Service	01/07/1916	31/07/1916
Heading	51st Divisional Artillery. 258th Brigade Royal Field Artillery August 1916		

War Diary In The Field 01/08/1916 22/08/1916

WO 95 2854/5

258 BRIGADE ROYAL FIELD ARTILLERY

1915 MAY - 1916 AUGUST 1916

51ST DIVISION

258TH (HIGHLAND) BDE RFA.
MAY 1915 - AUG 1916

BDE BROKEN UP

51st Division

12/6350

1/3 Highland Bde R.F.A.

Vol I.

1-5-3-7-14-

A₂
896

1/3rd Highland F.A. Bde. (How.)

Army Form C. 2118.

WAR DIARY

INTELLIGENCE SUMMARY
(Erase heading not required.)

1/3rd Bde. R.F.A. (How.)

Instructions regarding War Diaries and Intelligence Summaries are contained in F.S. Regs. Part II. and the Staff Manual respectively. Title pages will be prepared in manuscript.

Hour, Date, Place		Summary of Events and Information	Remarks and references to Appendices
May 1, 1915	BEDFORD	Mobilization preparations	
" 2	"	Ditto	
" 3	ON ACTIVE SERVICE	Entrained at BEDFORD; arrived SOUTHAMPTON; sailed for FRANCE.	
" 4	"	Arrived at HAVRE; entrained for front.	
" 5	"	Arrived at BERGUETTE; billetted at HAZINGHEM.	
" 6	"	Marched to find Billets at SAINT FLORIS.	
" 7	"	Subjects, reconnoitred.	
" 8	"	Ditto	
" 9	"	Ditto	
" 10	"	Arrived at FLEURBAIX; relieved Belgian positions near LACROIX MARECHAL.	
" 11	"	Ditto	
" 12	"	In action.	
" 13	"	In action.	
" 14	"	Ditto.	
" 15	"	Ditto.	
" 16	"	Ditto.	
" 17	"	Ditto.	
" 18	"	Ditto.	
" 19	"	Ditto.	
" 20	"	Ditto.	
" 21	"	Ditto.	
" 22	"	Ditto.	
" 23	"	Ditto.	
" 24	"	Ditto.	
" 25	"	Ditto.	
" 26	"	Bare position; right-hand.	
" 27	"	Arrive LOCON; relieve billets	
" 28	"	Points action on RUE DU BOIS.	
" 29	"	In action.	
" 30	"	Ditto.	
" 31	"	Ditto.	

Peter C. Macfarlane
LIEUT-COLONEL, R.F.A.
COMMANDING 1/3rd HIGHLAND F.A. (HOW.) BRIGADE.

1/2nd Highland F.A. Bde. (How.)

Army Form C. 2118.

WAR DIARY
INTELLIGENCE SUMMARY.
(Erase heading not required.)

Hour, Date, Place	Summary of Events and Information	Remarks and references to Appendices
June 1, 1915 — ON ACTIVE SERVICE	On action on RUE DU BOIS	
2	ditto	
3	ditto	
4	ditto	
5	ditto	
6	ditto	
7	ditto	
8	ditto	
9	ditto	
10	ditto	
11	ditto. 1 man wounded in 1/1st Ross-shire Battery R.F.A.	
12	ditto. 2 men wounded in 1/2nd Ross-shire Battery R.F.A.	
13	ditto	
14	Bombardment of German Trenches & redoubts opposite FESTUBERT.	
15	ditto	
16	Cessation of bombardment. Carry on with ordinary work.	
17	ditto	
18	Bombardment of German trenches & redoubts repeated	
19	Cessation of bombardment. Carry on with ordinary work.	
20	ditto	
21	ditto	
22	ditto	
23	ditto	
24	ditto	
25	ditto	
26	ditto	
27	ditto	
28	Night travel to position near LAVENTIE.	
29	On action near LAVENTIE.	
30	ditto	

30/6/75

Peter Macfarlane
LIEUT-COLONEL, R.F.A.
COMMANDING 1/2nd HIGHLAND F.A. (HOW.) BRIGADE.

1/3rd Highland F.A. Bde. (How.)

Army Form C. 2118.

WAR DIARY

INTELLIGENCE SUMMARY.

(Erase heading not required.)

Instructions regarding War Diaries and Intelligence Summaries are contained in F. S. Regs., Part II. and the Staff Manual respectively. Title pages will be prepared in manuscript.

Hour, Date, Place	Summary of Events and Information	Remarks and references to Appendices
1 July 1915 – On Active Service	In action near LAVENTIE.	
2 " "	ditto.	
3 " "	ditto.	
4 " "	ditto.	
5 " "	ditto.	
6 " "	ditto.	
7 " "	ditto.	
8 " "	ditto.	
9 " "	ditto.	
10 " "	ditto.	
11 " "	ditto.	
12 " "	ditto.	
13 " "	ditto.	
14 " "	ditto.	
15 " "	ditto.	
16 " "	ditto.	
17 " "	ditto.	
18 " "	ditto.	
19 " "	Marched by night near MERVILLE – where billeted.	
20 " "	Three lines ended ; consequent duties.	
21 " "	ditto.	
22 " "	ditto.	
23 " "	ditto.	
24 " "	ditto.	
25 " "	Marched by night to BERGUETTE, where entrained.	
26 " "	Arrived MÉRICOURT L'ABBÉ. Horse lines erected.	
27 " "	Examination of material etc.	
28 " "	ditto.	
29 " "	ditto.	
30 " "	ditto. Reparation of gun-positions near AVELUY.	
31 " "	ditto.	

Peter C. Macfarlane
LIEUT-COLONEL, R.F.A.
COMMANDING 1/3rd HIGHLAND F.A. (HOW) BRIGADE.

51st Division

121/6587

as art

1/3rd Highland Bde R.F.A.

Vol II

From 1 to 31.5.15

1/3RD HIGHLAND F.A. (HOW) BDE

Army Form C. 2118.

WAR DIARY
or
INTELLIGENCE SUMMARY.
(Erase heading not required.)

Instructions regarding War Diaries and Intelligence Summaries are contained in F. S. Regs., Part II. and the Staff Manual respectively. Title pages will be prepared in manuscript.

Hour, Date, Place	Summary of Events and Information	Remarks and references to Appendices
1 August 1915 On Active Service	Gunners preparing gun emplacements near AVELUY - Roads good Ground - Hilly & Woody, well watered & mostly of a limestone formation - D85 Battery attached to the Brigade	
2 — —	All Batteries in Action near AVELUY - Men in Shelter	
3 — —	Head Quarters arrived from MERICOURT at AVELUY & occupied house near the church	
4 — —	All Batteries in action near AVELUY	
5 — —	Do	
6 — —	Do	
7 — —	Do	
— —	Ammunition Columns left MERICOURT & arrived at WARLOY Men in Shelter - Country well wooded, but not so well watered as ALBERT district	
8 — —	All Batteries in Action near AVELUY Horse lines left MERICOURT & occupied new position at Mme DUVIVIER - Men in Shelters	

1/3RD HIGHLAND F.A. (HOW) BDE.

Army Form C. 2118.

WAR DIARY
or
INTELLIGENCE SUMMARY.
(Erase heading not required.)

Instructions regarding War Diaries and Intelligence Summaries are contained in F.S. Regs., Part II. and the Staff Manual respectively. Title pages will be prepared in manuscript.

Hour, Date, Place	Summary of Events and Information	Remarks and references to Appendices
8 August 1915 On Active Service	Head Quarters occupied new position vacated by French on the ALBERT side of AVELUY	
9 — —	All Batteries in action near AVELUY	
10 — —	Do	
11 — —	Do	
12 — —	Do	
— —	Severe thunder & lightning storm, accompanied by heavy rain	
13 — —	All Batteries in action near AVELUY	
14 — —	Do	
14 — —	Leave commenced. German plane passed overhead & dropped bombs in the marshes	
15 — —	All Batteries in action near AVELUY	
16 — —	1st Battery in conjunction with 6"(How) Batteries shelled LA BOISELLE — Shooting effective. Barometer received. Weather fine with occasional showers Barometer 29-9-7	

(9 29 6) W 2794 100,000 5/14 H W V Forms/C. 2118/11

1/3RD HIGHLAND F.A. (HOW) BDE WAR DIARY or INTELLIGENCE SUMMARY.
(Erase heading not required.)

Army Form C. 2118.

Hour, Date, Place	Summary of Events and Information	Remarks and references to Appendices
17 August 1915 On Active Service	All Batteries in action near AVELUY. 1st Battery attached to 83RD BDE RFA & 2nd Battery attached to 1st Highland Bde R.F.A. for tactical purposes. Administration still carried on by their own headquarters. D85 Battery left the Brigade & attached to Indian Cavalry R.H.A. Albert slightly shelled. Weather fine as found. Barometer 29-9-3.	
18 — — —	Both Batteries in action near AVELUY. Weather dull & showery. Barometer 29-9-6 Wind N.	
19 — — —	Both Batteries in action near AVELUY - Wind N. Weather fine occasional showers. Barometer 29-9-6 In evening Engineers exploded a mine in the front of the trenches. 1st Battery in conjunction with other Batteries opened fire immediately the mine was exploded - shooting effective. Weather as above.	
20 — — —	Both Batteries in action near AVELUY - Weather fine Wind NW. Barometer 30-10	

1/3RD HIGHLAND F.A. (HOW) BDE

Army Form C. 2118.

WAR DIARY
or
INTELLIGENCE SUMMARY.
(Erase heading not required.)

Instructions regarding War Diaries and Intelligence Summaries are contained in F.S. Regs., Part II. and the Staff Manual respectively. Title pages will be prepared in manuscript.

Place	Date	Hour	Summary of Events and Information	Remarks and references to Appendices
On Active Service	21/8/15	—	Both Batteries in Action near AVELUY — Barometer 30.05 Wind NW Weather bright with dull intervals	
Do	22/8/15	—	Do	Do — 30.07 — N.W. Do	
Do	23/8/15	—	Do	Do 30.28 — N.W. Do	
Do	24/8/15	—	Do	Do 30.16 — N. Bright sunshine very close	
Do	25/8/15	—	Do	Do 30.10 — N.E. Do	
Do	26/8/15	—	Do	Do 30.05 — N.E. Do	
Do	27/8/15	—	Do	Do 29.75 — N.E. Do	
Do	28/8/15	—	Do	Do 29.68 — N. Bright, Rain Thunder lightning in evening	
Do	29/8/15	—	Do	Do 29.70 — N. Dull, Bright intervals	
Do	30/8/15	—	Do	Do 29.70 — N. —	
Do	31/8/15	—	Do	Do 30.06 — N. —	

1/3RD HIGHLAND F.A. (HOW.) BDE. 31 AUG. 1915

LIEUT-COLONEL, R.F.A.
COMMANDING 1/3rd HIGHLAND F.A. (HOW.) BRIGADE.

51/6918

51st Division

1/3. Highland Bde R. F. A.
Vol III
Sept. 15

1/3rd High. F.A. (How) Bde

WAR DIARY
or
INTELLIGENCE SUMMARY.

Army Form C. 2118.

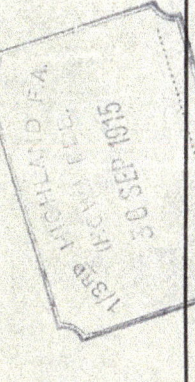

Place	Date	Hour	Summary of Events and Information	Remarks and references to Appendices
AVELUY	1/9/15 to 9/9/15		Both Batteries in Action near AVELUY	
do	10/9/15		In the evening the 2nd Battery in conjunction with the 1st High. F.A. Bde shelled the enemies transport, causing great panic, at Crossroads OVILLIERS LA BOISELLE. The road has not since been used for transport. In action near AVELUY	
do	11/9/15 to 12/9/15		In action near AVELUY.	
do	13/9/15		Albert heavily shelled. By the base of a shell it was found that 155 m.m. guns, captured from the French, were used. — Aeroplane (German) overhead, pursued by British machine but escaped. — B. Hazlewood No 723 Gunshot wound in thigh — In action near AVELUY In action near AVELUY	
do	14/9/15		German plane overhead forced to return by our anti-aircraft guns. In action near AVELUY	
do	15/9/15		ALBERT & AVELUY both slightly shelled — In action near AVELUY	
do	16/9/15 to 17/9/15		In action near AVELUY	
do	18/9/15		Two German planes overhead — Shelled by anti-aircraft guns — In action near AVELUY	
do	19/9/15		Horse & Wagon lines left Moulin du Vivier & proceeded to BRESLE — Do	
do	20/9/15		German plane attacked by British one — forced to descend in German lines — Do a lot of work done by Germans at point 408 (Ref. Maps. 2 Bis 1/20000) — 2nd Battery in conjunction with 4·7" & 4·5" Batteries fired on it, with satisfactory results the work being badly damaged.	

1/3rd High. F.A. (How) Bde

Army Form C. 2118.

WAR DIARY
or
INTELLIGENCE SUMMARY.
(Erase heading not required.)

Place	Date	Hour	Summary of Events and Information	Remarks and references to Appendices
AVELUY	20/9/15		In action near AVELUY - ALBERT heavily shelled 5.2" shells being much	
	21/9/15		In action near AVELUY	
	22/9/15		An aerial duel took place - the German forces to descent, but reached German lines. Both sections	
			1st Batty took up new position to North of AVELUY - owing to 18th Div taking over part of our line	
	23/9/15		Bombardment started. All Batteries on our front engaged - Very little retaliation - Flight of	
			114 aeroplanes passed over to attack VALENCIENNES STATION - Severe thunder storm in evening	
	24/9/15		Bombardment continued	
	25/9/15		Do - Do	
	26/9/15		In action near Aveluy.	
	27/9/15		Do	
	28/9/15		Do	
	29/9/15		Do	
	30/9/15		Do German plane brought down by British plane - Both airmen (Germans) killed.	

Peter Macfarlane LIEUT-COLONEL R.F.A.
COMMANDING 1/3rd HIGHLAND F.A. (HOW) BRIGADE.

121/7333

51st Divn

1/3rd Highland Bde R.F.A.

Vol IV

Oct. 15

Army Form C. 2118.

1/3RD HIGH. F.A. (Now) BDE

WAR DIARY
or
INTELLIGENCE SUMMARY.

(Erase heading not required.)

Instructions regarding War Diaries and Intelligence Summaries are contained in F.S. Regs., Part II. and the Staff Manual respectively. Title pages will be prepared in manuscript.

Stamp: 1/3RD HIGHLAND F.A. (HOW) BDE. 31 OCT 1915

Place	Date	Hour	Summary of Events and Information	Remarks and references to Appendices
AVELUY	1/10/15		In action near AVELUY – This front very quiet. Major General G.M. Harper C.B. D.S.O. the new G.O.C. visited & inspected the horselines	
	2/10/15		Do – Aerial firing observed at 8.45 p.m, but no aeroplane was seen	
	3/10/15		Do – Two hostile planes tried to cross our lines, but were driven back by our anti-aircraft guns.	
	4/10/15		Do	
	9/10/15		Do	
	10/10/15		Do – Hostile aeroplane again busy. Repelled by our anti-aircraft guns	
	11/10/15		Do – Two search lights were observed sending up perpendicular rays.	
	12/10/15		Do	
	20/10/15		Do	
	21/10/15		Do – Two additional Officers joined (Lieut Mannel & 2/Lt McLean)	
	22/10/15		Do – On 25th His Majesty King George V visited the Corps (10th Corps)	
	25/10/15		Do – Hostile aeroplanes again active	
	26/10/15		Do	
	27/10/15		Do	
	28/10/15		Do – Bombardment of certain points in German trenches by both batteries in conjunction with the rest of the artillery in the Divisional	
	29/10/15		Do – Aveluy shelled.	
	30/10/15		Do – During this month both batteries were mostly engaged in retaliation on Trench Mortars – The 2nd Battery is still attached to the 1st High. F.A. Bde. for Tactical purposes. – ALBERT is shelled almost nightly, but only a few shells are sent each night. The front here very quiet during the whole month.	

Robt. Chuckerbury (?) Lt. Colonel
Commanding 1/3 High. F.A. (How) Bde

Perforated Sheet giving detail of personnel and horses wanting to complete, shown on Army Form B. 213.

Number of Report 22

Detail of Wanting to Complete	Drivers R.A.	Drivers R.E.	Drivers A.S.C.	Drivers Car	Drivers Lorry	Drivers Steam	Gunners	Smith Gunners	Range Takers	Farriers Sergeants	Farriers Corporals	Shoeing, or Shoeing and Carriage Smiths	Cold Shoers	Wheelers R.A.	Wheelers H.T.	Wheelers M.T.	Saddlers or Harness Makers	Blacksmiths	Bricklayers and Masons	Carpenters and Joiners	Fitters & Turners (R.E.) Wood	Fitters & Turners (R.E.) Iron	Fitters R.A.	Fitters Wireless	Plumbers	Electricians Ordinary	Electricians W.T.	Signalmen	Engine Drivers Loco.	Engine Drivers Field	Air Line Men	Permanent Line Men	Operators, Telegraph	Cablemen	Brigade Section Pioneers	General-duty Pioneers	Signallers	Instrument Repairers	Motor Cyclists	Motor Cyclist Artificers	Telephonists	Clerks	Machine Gunners	Armament Artificers Fitters	Armament Artificers Range Finders	Armourers	Storemen	Privates	W.O's. and N.C.O's. (by ranks) not included in trade columns	TOTAL, wanting to complete Officers	TOTAL Other Ranks	Horses Riding	Horses Draught	Horses Heavy Draught	Horses Pack
CAVALRY																																																						
R.A.	29						19					1		1			1																																	2	3		52		6	1
R.E.																																																								
INFANTRY																																																1								
R.A.M.C.																																																				1				
A.O.C.																																																								
A.V.C.																																																								

Remarks: — *[handwritten notes, partially legible]* ...the shortage of men is very serious but ... reported shortage except those of smiths, saddlers & transport could be spread out by Brigade ...

Signature of Commander: *W.S. Chieftainure* LIEUT. COLONEL R.F.A
COMMANDING 1ST RESERVE FIELD ARTILLERY BRIGADE
Unit: F. Corps.
Formation to which attached:
Date of Despatch: 3.9.15

Army Form B. 213.

FIELD RETURN.

No. of Report. 22

(To be furnished by all arms, services, and departments (except A.S.C. units) to the A. G.'s Office at the Base in accordance with Field Service Regulations, Part II.)

RETURN showing numbers RATIONED by, and Transport on charge of, 1/3rd High La Corps at 3rd October 19 15. Date.

DETAIL	Personnel			Animals							Guns, carriages, and limbers and transport vehicles									REMARKS
	Officers	Other ranks	Natives	Horses Riding	Horses Draught	Horses Heavy Draught	Pack	Mules Large	Mules Small	Camels	Oxen	Guns, carriages, limbers, showing description	Ammunition wagons and limbers	Machine Guns	Aircraft, showing description	Horsed 4 Wheeled	Horsed 2 Wheeled	Motor Cars	Tractors	Mechanical Lorries, showing description	Mechanical Trucks, showing description	Trailers	Motor Bicycles	Bicycles	
Effective Strength of Unit	19	464		157	193			90				2 B.L. 5 inch	37 1 Ex. Wag. 16 R.T.C. bows			1	9							4	Included 1 officer & 9 other ranks attached from Canadian until end Sept.
Details, by Corps attached to unit as in War Establishment:—																									
R.A.M.C.	1	2		1																					One horse + groom just arrived.
A.V.C.	1	1		2																					
A.O.C.		1																							
Interp.	1			1																					1 horse transferred
Civil.																									
Total	19	460		141	193			90				2 B.L. 5 inch	37			1	9							4	
War Establishment	19	518		143	190			90								4	9							4	4 Officers not mustered & 2 more August
Wanting to complete (Detail of Personnel and Horses below)		58		2	7							8				3									1/3 How. excess G. Estobbell (17)
Surplus																									
*Attached (not to include the details shown above)		1																							
Civilians:— Employed with the Unit Accompanying the Unit																									Reports does not incur Return
TOTAL RATIONED	19	391		141	193			90																	

* In the case of field ambulances, hospitals or depots, the number of patients are to be included here, the names being shown in A. F. A. 36.

John Macfarlane LIEUT.-COLONEL, R.F.A.
Signature of Commander.
COMMANDING 1/3rd HIGHLAND BDE. R.F.A.
30th October 1915.
Date of Despatch.

For information of the A.G.'s Office at the Base.

Officers and men who have become casuals, been transferred or joined since last report.

Place: On Active Service Date: 30.X.15

Regtl. Number	Rank	Name	Corps	Nature of casualty, or name of unit from or to which transferred	Date of being struck off or coming on the ration return	Remarks*
7244	Gr	Taylor. A	Hd Qrs	Awarded 28 days F.P. No 2	23.X.15	Offence — Conduct to the prejudice of good order & military discipline
1213	D	Hastings. A	1st Renfrew (4) Bty	To Fd Amb	22.X.15	
683	Gr	Murray. J	— do —	From — .. —	25.X.15	
903	D	Purdie. J	— do —		27.X.15	
690	Bdr	Weller. B	— do —	Prom: Bomb	22.X.15	vice Baillie
877	Bdr	Grant. B	— do —	Appt a/Bdr	17.X.15	" Bain
936	D	Cummings. Ja	— do —		22.X.15	" Weller
446	Sn/Sgt	Little. Ja	— do —	Prom: A.M.F.Sgt.	20.X.15	To complete estb
692	D	Boyd. H	— do —	Appt F.Smith	20.X.15	— do —
169	Lgt	Russell. J R	— do —	7 days leave	27.X.15	To U.K
1197	Gr	Wilkinson. JR	— do —		27.X.15	
805	D	Franklin. W	2nd Renfrew (4) Bty	To Fd Amb	20.X.15	
848	Gr	Feeny. W	— do —		22.X.15	
1026	"	McDowell. C	— do —		22.X.15	
776	"	Griffin. W	— do —		27.X.15	
805	D	Hinksley. W	— do —	From — .. —	25.X.15	
471	"	Kyle. J	— do —		27.X.15	
1075	"	Murray. Y	— do —	7 days leave	24.X.15	To U.K
435	Sgt	McKirdy	— do —		27.X.15	— .. —
441	Cpl	Kerr. M	— do —	— .. —	27.X.15	— .. —
903	Gr	Tweedale. R	— do —	Mustered Gr	28.X.15	
599	Sh/Smth	Stewart. R	Amm Column	Allotn 9d	6.X.15	
521	Bdr	Stark. R	— do —	— .. — 6d	9.X.15	
1139	Gr	Mitchell. R	— do —	Trangd F.Amb	24.X.15	
1080	D	Brown. J	— do —	To Fd Amb	24.X.15	
790	G	Bodie. M	— do —	From — .. —	28.X.15	
441	Gr	Stewart. J	— do —	Awarded 6 days F.P. No 2	26.X.15	
597	D	Rattray. J	— do —			
406	Cpl	Campbell. W	— do —	7 days leave	27.X.15	To U.K
273	Sgt	Smith. Y	Renfrew Ed	— .. —	27.X.15	
662	Gr	Haliburton. A	Renfrew Architecture	Transfd to Amm Column	24.X.15	
1100	"	O'Neill. J	Architecture	To Base Depot	25.X.15	For Dental treatment

* State whether absence is of a permanent or temporary nature, adding, in the case of casuals from wounds or disease, any available information for communication to the relatives.

121/7637

51st Division

1/3rd Highland Bde R.F.A.

Nov. 1915

Vol V

1/3rd High F.A. (How) Bde.

Army Form C. 2118.

WAR DIARY
or
INTELLIGENCE SUMMARY.

(Erase heading not required.)

Place	Date	Hour	Summary of Events and Information	Remarks and references to Appendices
Aveluy AVELUY	1-11-15	—	Some shells were dug up (which had been fired on 30th Sept) & were found to be 6·1" French shells from 155 m.m gun thought to be captured from the French at Maubeuge. Both Batteries in action near Aveluy. — German incendiary shells fired at Aveluy	(AVELUY)
—	2-11-15		Do.	
—	4-11-15		Do.	
—	5-11-15		Do.	
—	6-11-15		Do. — Hostile Battery located by French Map 2 Bts. between front 424 + 6111	
—	7-11-15		Do. — Head Qrs left Aveluy took up new Billets in Albert	(ALBERT)
—	8-11-15		Do.	
—	11-11-15		Both Batteries in conjunction with other Brigades had a small bombardment of the German lines today, shooting very effective — a number of parties of Germans were observed on the POZIER — CONTAL MAISON ROAD — One of the walls of THIEPVAL CHATEAU was either taken down — 20 shells fired into ALBERT.	
—	12-11-15		Both Batteries in action near AVELUY — 14 shells fired into ALBERT.	
—	13-11-15		Do. — Lieut J.D. Adam joined Brigade	
—	14-11-15		Do.	
—	16-11-15		Do.	
—	17-11-15		1 Section of D85 Battery took over from 2nd Renfrew Batty.	
—	18-11-15		1st Renfrew Batty + Right Section of 2nd Renfrew Batty in action near Aveluy — D85 Registered	
—	20-11-15		Left Section of 2nd Renfrew Batty proceeded to BRESLE	
—	21-11-15		1 Section of 1/4th London Batty (111th Brigade) took over from D 85	
—	22-11-15			
—	23-11-15		Remaining section of 1/4th London Batty relieved Right section of 2nd Renfrew Batty — 2nd Renfrew proceeded to BRESLE	
—	24-11-15			
—	25-11-15			
—	26-11-15		1st Batty in action near AVELUY.	
—	27-11-15		During the month things were very quiet on this front — Head Qrs in Billets — 2nd Battery in dugouts until 26th — now in huts at BRESLE	1st Batty in BRESLE
—	30-11-15			

LIEUT-COLONEL R.F.A.
COMMANDING 1/3rd HIGHLAND F.A. (HOWITZER)

FIELD RETURN.

Army Form B. 213.

No. of Report 26

(To be furnished by all arms, services, and departments (except A.S.C. units) to the A. G.'s Office at the Base in accordance with Field Service Regulations, Part II.)

RETURN showing numbers RATIONED by, and Transport on charge of 13th Highland Fd (Hd) Brigade. Date 24th Nov 1915.

DETAIL.	Personnel			Animals.							Guns, carriages, and limbers and transport vehicles				Mechanical					REMARKS
	Officers	Other ranks	Natives	Horses Riding	Horses Draught	Horses Heavy Draught	Mules Pack	Mules Large	Mules Small	Camels	Oxen	Guns, carriages and limbers, showing description	Ammunition wagons and limbers	Machine Guns	Aircraft, showing description	Horsed 4 Wheeled	Horsed 2 Wheeled	Motor Cars	Tractors	Lorries, showing description	Trucks, showing description	Trailers	Motor Bicycles	Bicycles	
Effective Strength of Unit	19	389	—	13	197	—	—	91	—	—	—	8	34			1	9							4	x Includes 2 Officers, 22 Other ranks on leave, 8 sick
Details, by Arms attached to unit as in War Establishment:— R.A.M.C. A.V.C. A.O.C. Interpreter A.S.C.	1 1 1	3 2 1		1 2 1	2											3									Train Transport
Total	19	393	—	14	199	—	—	91	—	—	—	8	34			4	9							4	
War Establishment	20	458	—	14	290	—	—	—	—	—	—	8	34			1	9							4	Does not include Train transport
Wanting to complete	1	65	—	—	91	—	—																		3 Officers in excess of authorised establishment
Surplus								91																	1 Officer in Field Ambulance (Major Robertson)
*Attached (not to include the details shown above)		49																							Interpreter does not draw Rations
Civilians:— Employed with the Unit Accompanying the Unit																									
TOTAL RATIONED	19	443	—	14	199	—	—	91	—	—	—														

* In the case of field ambulances, hospitals or depots, the number of patients are to be included here, the names being shown in A. F. A. 36.

Signature of Commander. Lewis Capt for Colonel, R.F.A. Commanding 13th Highland Brigade

Date of Despatch 24th Nov 1915.

Perforated Sheet giving detail of personnel and horses wanting to complete, shown on Army Form B. 213.

Number of Report __26__

Detail of Wanting to Complete	Drivers						Gunners	Smith Gunners	Range Takers	Farriers		Shoeing, or Carriage Smiths	Cold Shoers	Wheelers			Saddlers or Harness Makers	Blacksmiths	Bricklayers and Masons	Carpenters and Joiners	Fitters & Turners (R.E.)		Wireless	R.A.	Plumbers	Electricians		Signalmen	Engine Drivers		Air Line Men	Permanent Line Men	Operators, Telegraph	Cablemen	Brigade Section Pioneers	General-duty Pioneers	Signallers	Instrument Repairers	Motor Cyclists	Motor Cyclist Artificers	Telephonists	Clerks	Machine Gunners	Armament Artificers				Stretchermen	Privates	W.O's and N.C.O's (by ranks) not included in trade columns	TOTAL wanting to complete to agree with		Horses			
	R.A.	R.E.	A.S.C.	Car	Lorry	Steam				Serjeants	Corporals			R.A.	H.T.	M.T.					Wood	Iron				Ordinary	W.T.		Loco.	Field														Fitters	Range Finders	Armourers					Officers	Other Ranks	Riding	Draught	Heavy Draught	Pack
CAVALRY																																																								
R.A.	29						29							1			2																																		Saddlers 2,2	3	64×2,2		4×2,2		Pack mules
R.E.																																																								
INFANTRY																																																								
R.A.M.C.																																													1						1					
A.O.C.																																																								
A.V.C.																																																								

× Officers charges for medium weight.

Remarks:— Appointments & Promotions except those of Saddlers & Trumpeters will be filled up in Brigade.

The Brigade is still 65 men under strength. Our monthly returns of casualties & reinforcements 18/15

Signature of Commander. Officer Cmdg. Capt. [signature]

Formation to which attached. Xth Bde.

Unit. _____

Date of Despatch. 24th Nov 1915

1/3rd Highland Bde R.F.A. (How?)

Sec ———
Vol. VI

50 ¢

1/3rd High F.A. (How) 13de WAR DIARY or INTELLIGENCE SUMMARY.

Army Form C. 2118.

Place	Date	Hour	Summary of Events and Information	Remarks and references to Appendices
AVELUY			POSITION REF. TRENCH MAP 1/20000 57D SE IIeEDITION. — 1st BATTY — W11a-4·4 — 2nd BATTY W11b-7-8. NEW POSITION OF 1st BTY = D0 — Q34a-4·7.	
	11-12-15	at 1a.	1st Battery in action near AVELUY. — Very quiet on this front.	
	12-12-15		— - — - — - — 2nd Batty returned from Breale took up original position	
	23-12-15		Both Batteries — - — - — Nothing worthy of reporting happens	
	24-12-15		— - — - — in conjunction with 8" How, 6"Guns, & 4-5"How had a shoot today. a great deal of damage was done to the enemies trenches wire & a shelter evidently containing ammunition was blown up.	
	25-12-15		ALBERT was shelled with small high velocity Shrapnel & H.E.	
	26-12-15		Both Batteries in action near Aveluy	
	27-12-15		Do	
	28-12-15		Do — In conjunction with (8"How) 6"Guns & 4-5"How had a shoot today during which considerable damage was done to the enemies trenches. 1st Batty	
	29/12/15		Do — Right section of 1st Bty went to new position north of MESNIL.	
	30/12/15		Do — 1st Battery took part in bombardment of enemies trenches	
	31/12/15			

W. Macfarlane Lt Colonel
Commanding 1/3 Highlan (H) Bde

1/3rd Heigh? Bde R.F.A.
Jan 1916
Vol. VII

1/3rd High. J.A.(N) B.M.

WAR DIARY
or
INTELLIGENCE SUMMARY.

Army Form C. 2118.

Place	Date	Hour	Summary of Events and Information	Remarks and references to Appendices
ALBERT	8/1/16		2nd Battery left AVELUY & proceeded to Bresle	
-	9/1/16 to 10/1/16		1st Bty in action near MESNIL during this time their billets were heavily shelled & some large shells landed near the Gun position	
ALBERT	3/1/16		Head Quarters left ALBERT & proceeded to WARLOY BALLION	
WARLOY	7/1/16		do WARLOY do proceeded to ST SAUVEUR	
ST SAUVEUR	9/1/16		2nd Battery left BRESLE & do do do	
do	11/1/16		Ammunition Column left WARLOY do do do	
do	12/1/16		1st Bty left MESNIL & proceeded to BRESLE	
do	12/1/16		do do BRESLE do do ST SAUVEUR	
do	10/1/16		On this day the Brigade were rearmed with the 4.5 equipment	
do	29/1/16		Gun Drill, Fatigues &c. for Brigade	
do	31/1/16		Inspection of Horses Harness by Brigadier General McCritty	

Otto C Macfarlane LIEUT-COLONEL R.F.A.
COMMANDING 1/3rd HIGHLAND HOWR BRIGADE.

NOTE OF AMMUNITION FIRED.

		A.	AX.	BX.		A.	AX.	BX.
13th.	10 a.m.	255 Bde. 5479	584	759	161 Bde. 4003	1021	823
	6 p.m.	" 1124	626	260	" 281	844	Nil.
14th.	10 a.m.	" 2322	198	517	" 1586	667	512
	6 p.m.	" 748	Nil.	156	" 792	464	36
15th.	10 a.m.	" 1964	355	150	" ...	Nil	...
	6 p.m.	" 1468	834	...	" 21	60	24
16th.	10 a.m.	" 323	151	...	" 404	168	70
	6 p.m.	" 403	...	...	" 34	12	12
17th.	10 a.m.	" 102	76	...	" 192	135	70.
		13,933.	2824.	1842.	7313	3371	1547
		Total 18,599.			Total 12,231.		

1/31st High. F.A.(H) Bde

WAR DIARY
or
INTELLIGENCE SUMMARY.
(Erase heading not required.)

Army ...

Instructions regarding War Diaries and Intelligence Summaries are contained in F. S. Regs, Part II. and the Staff Manual respectively. Title pages will be prepared in manuscript.

Place	Date	Hour	Summary of Events and Information	Remarks and references to Appendices
ST SAUVEUR	16/3/16	–	Colonel Macfarlane, Capt Wallock v Sergt McGhee were mentioned in despatches on 11/1/16.	
	17/3/16	–	Brigade resting at St Sauveur – Gun drill, Riding Drill &c	
	18/3/16	–	Brigade left for BUSSY LES DAOURS arriving there on the same day. A Battery T.H.S. (Hows) joined the brigade from 151st Brigade 30th Div. & is now known as the 3rd Battery	
	19/3/16		Brigade resting at BUSSY LES DAOURS – Usual Routine	
	23/3/16			
	24/3/16		– began to move to forward area at Bray & Suzanne, relieving the 151st Brigade	
	26/3/16		Move completed & all batteries in action – Bray heavily shelled 5 men being killed & about 8 wounded, also six horses killed, all of various batteries in action	
	27/3/16		All three Batteries in action	
	28/3/16		Brigade moved to back area at Bussy les Daours being relieved by the 151st Brigade	
	29/3/16		Brigade moved from Bussy les Daours to Villers Bocage	

John C Macfarlane, LIEUT-COLONEL R.F.A.
COMMANDING 1/3rd HIGHLAND (HOW) BRIGADE

1/3RD HIGH. F.A. (H) BDE.

WAR DIARY or INTELLIGENCE SUMMARY

Army Form C. 2118.

Place	Date	Hour	Summary of Events and Information	Remarks and references to Appendices
VILLERS BOCAGE	1/3/16		Brigade rested in Villers Bocage	
Do	5/3/16		left Villers Bocage for HEM arriving the same night	
HEM	6/3/16		rested in HEM	
Do	7/3/16		left HEM for REBREUVIETTE arriving the same night	
Do	8/3/16		rested in REBREUVIETTE	
REBREUVIETTE	9/3/16			
Do	10/3/16		left REBREUVIETTE for AGNEZ LEZ DUISANS arriving the same night. 1st & 2nd Bty Battery took up a position near ANZIN. 1st BTY. REF. MAP SIGNE (B.Series) F30 a 6-9 — 2nd Dº REF MAP 51B N.W. 1/20000 A 25 b 2-7 — Both Batteries in action	
Do			R Battery took up position REF. MAP SIGNE 20000 (B Series) F 30 a-6-7. All Batteries in action Wagon Lines & Column left AGNEZ LES DUISANS for FREVIN CAPELLE	
Do	12/3/16		All Batteries in action 1 Bty attached to 1/1st High. J.A. (H) Bde, 2nd Dº to 1/2 Lowland Bde	
Do	14/3/16		R. Att. to 1/3rd High. J.A.(Bde) for tactical purposes	
Do	15/3/16		1st Battery heavily shelled with 8" shells. 3 men killed & turned with a shell	
Do	20/3/16			
G.H.Q. Bn Train	30/3/16		— — no casualties. was at time of writing	
Do	31/3/16		1st ASFg no again heavy shelled	

51

1/3 High Bde R.F.A

Vol X

1/3 High St

1/3RD HIGH. F.A.(HOW) Bde

WAR DIARY
or
INTELLIGENCE SUMMARY.
(Erase heading not required.)

Army Form C. 2118.

Instructions regarding War Diaries and Intelligence Summaries are contained in F. S. Regs., Part II. and the Staff Manual respectively. Title pages will be prepared in manuscript.

1/3RD HIGHLAND F.A. (HOW) BDE.
2 MAY 1916

Place	Date	Hour	Summary of Events and Information	Remarks and references to Appendices
Maroeuil	1/4/16		All Batteries in action in same position as last month.	
do	2/4/16		Lieut Russell & 2/Lt Husband 3/3rd Lowland F.A. Bde joined the Brigade from the 3/3rd Lowland F.A. Bde. All Batteries in action	
do	3/4/16		2/Lt Robertson (from 2/3rd High F.A.(H) Bde on a 14 days course) arrived today. All Batteries in action	
do	4/4/16, 5/4/16, 6/4/16		2/Lt Baillie joined the Brigade from 3/3rd High. F.A.(H) Bde. All Btys in action	
do	7/4/16		2/Lt Husband to Field Ambulance. All Batteries in action	
do	8/4/16, 9/4/16, 10/4/16		All Batteries in action	
do	11/4/16		Lieut Manuel slightly wounded. All Batteries in action	
do	12/4/16		1st Bty. heavily shelled with 8 2" Armour piercing Shells. No Casualties	
do	13/4/16, 14/4/16, 20/4/16		All Batteries in action	
do	21/4/16		2/Lt A.A. Moir joined the Brigade from 3/3rd High F.A.(H) Bde. All Batteries in action	
do	22/4/16 to 27/4/16		All Batteries in action	
do	28/4/16	6.30 p.m	Do Do Do In evening a combined shoot took place. Heavy Bty 6b" + 4.5" guns taking part. The shoot was most successful, great damage being done by Muir cottages in the front line. Artillery opened an intense barrage.	
do	29/4/16	2 a.m.	German plane fell close to our position. Both Airmen killed.	
do	29/4/16	9.48 a.m.	A German plane was brought down & forced to descent by our anti-aircraft	
do	30/4/16	7.30 a.m	guns. A Combined shoot similar to that of 25th took place tonight	

Peter C. Macfarlane LIEUT-COLONEL R.F.A.
COMMANDING 1/3rd HIGHLAND F.A. (HOW) BDE.

Headquarters 258th Bde R.F.A.

258 Bde RFA
Army Form C. 2118.

WAR DIARY
or
INTELLIGENCE SUMMARY.

Place	Date	Hour	Summary of Events and Information	Remarks and references to Appendices
	1/5/16 to 16/5/16	—	All three Batteries of 4.5" Hows in action at old position	
	17/5/16	—	On this date owing to the reorganisation of the artillery, the 3"" High T.A. (HOW) Bde was done away with. The 1st Renfrew Battery joined the 255th Bde, the 2nd Renfrew Bty joined the 260th Bde "R" Batty joined the 256th Bde. The Headquarters were made the HQ of the 258th Bde which was composed of D Battery of the 1st Highland, D Battery of the 2nd Highland, & D Battery of the Lowland where known as A Bty B/258 & C/258 respectively. On this date the 51st Div Artillery took down from 25th Div. A/258 changed over with B/110 taking over their guns & occupied a position at A 26d 3/0. B/258 took up a position at g.3a 3/6 v C/258 at a 13d 9/5. Reference Map 1/20000 51CNE (B series)	
	06/5/16 to 28/5/16	—	On the 25th Div taking over again C/258 moved to a new position at g.2c 75/10. Head Quarters moved to FREVIN CAPELLE C/258 again moved back to position at g.2a 75/10.	
	29/5/16 to 30/5/16	—	During the month things were fairly quiet on this front but on 21/5/16 there was heavy fighting on our left & the germans used a large quantity of gas shells, & took some trenches	

R Wilson Lt.

258th Bde R.F.A. WAR DIARY or INTELLIGENCE SUMMARY
(Erase heading not required.)

Army Form C. 2118

258 Bde RFA

Place	Date	Hour	Summary of Events and Information	Remarks and references to Appendices
Near ANZIN	1/6/16		All 3 Batteries in action near ANZIN Reference trench map 51 b. N.W. A/258 Bty at G3 a 1-7, B/258 Bty at G3 a 3-5 C/258 Bty at A13 d 9-5	
	2/6/16		Lieut Dunningham to hospital, all Batteries in action	
	3/5/16 to 16/6/16		All Batteries in action. Nothing special to report.	
	16/6/16		B/258 were heavily shelled 4 men being wounded	
	17/6/16 to 26/6/16		All Batteries in action. Do.	
	27/6/16 28/6/16		4 days Bombardment of the German lines in which A/258 & B/258 took part. The shooting was very effective & caused certain damage to the enemies trenches, wire &c. On the 29/6/16 the infantry let off clouds of smoke the artillery bombarded the enemies trenches. As the Germans manned the trenches a large number of casualties were known to have been caused. Lieut Thorpe joined Bde on 27/6/16	
	1/6/16 29/6/16		All Btries in action — Lieut Nicol rejoined 256" Bde R F A. During the month a number of mines were put up both by the Germans & ourselves, also several enemy raids but not of much importance, our infantry also made some very successful raids	

Peter Charteleman Lieut Colonel

CONFIDENTIAL.
No 309/A
HIGHLAND DIVISION.

Vol 13

Confidential

War Diary

of

258th Brigade R.F.A.
Shown as 257 Bde

from 1st July 1916 to 31st July 1916

(Volume)

Army Form C. 2118.

WAR DIARY
or
INTELLIGENCE SUMMARY of 258th BRIGADE R.F.A. No 309/A HIGHLAND DIVISION

(Erase heading not required.)

Place	Date	Hour	Summary of Events and Information	Remarks and references to Appendices
On Active Service	1/7/16 to 14/7/16		Batteries in action in LABYRINTH Sector. Headquarters at FREVIN-CAPELLE. Batteries grouped with other Brigades. On night of 14th/15th Batteries moved out of action to FREVIN-CAPELLE	WD34.
	15/7/16		Brigade moved to LUCHEUX. Trek about 17 miles.	WD34
	16/7/16		Brigade moved to HEUZECOURT and remained	WD34
	17/7/16 to 19/7/16		till night of 19/7/16 when it moved to HAVERNAS	WD34
	20/7/16 21/7/16		Brigade moved to PERNANCOURT and remained till night of 23rd when Brigade	WD34 WD34
	23/7/16	10PM	moved in to action. Registration of zones carried out. Heavy barrage put up by B25 at night on report + order WD34 from 51st(H)DA that German infantry was advancing on either side of HIGH WOOD, by Caterpillar WD34	WD34
	24/7/16		BRIGADE all guns in action near CATERPILLAR WOOD	
	25/7/16		Liaison commenced with 154th INFANTRY BDE. Hqrs of B25, A.B.C Batteries heavily shelled HIGH WOOD	WD34
			LIEUT G.A.D. McDONALD slightly wounded. 6 men wounded. OO.34.) 154th Bde attack	
	26/7/16		Valley heavily shelled by Enemy with gas shells till 4AM 51st(H)DA 2 men slightly gassed. Enemy	WD34
			commenced shelling with gas shells at 10PM	
	27/7/16		Enemy continued to shell valley with gas shells till 5AM. Capt J.H. EDWARDS gas casualty	WD34
			3 men wounded on this day. Heavy barrage by enemy on valley. OO 35.51st(H)DA Infantry	WD34
			on night attack + capture LONGUEVAL + DELVILLE WOOD V right	
	28/7/16		Batteries in action. 2 men wounded and One man killed	WD34
	29/7/16		OO 36.51st(H)DA Brigade shells trenches on right of HIGH WOOD	WD34
	30/7/16		OO. 37. 51st(H)DA Repetition of OO.36. Only ammunition expenditure greater. OO 38. 51st(H)DA Infantry attack WOOD LANE. Heavy barrage put up over valley by enemy on this day. Capt F.B. McKINLAY admitted into Hospital sick. F.O.O.	WD34 WD34

WAR DIARY or INTELLIGENCE SUMMARY

of 258th BRIGADE R.F.A

Army Form C. 2118.

Place	Date	Hour	Summary of Events and Information	Remarks and references to Appendices
On active Service	3/7/16		Brigade in action 19th Division Division on our left 5th Division Division on our right Hqrs in position at S 20 c 5.5 (Ref T M 57c SW 3) A/258 in position at S 20 c 4.5 (do) B/258 in position at S 20 d 3.5 (do) C/258 in position at S 20 C 5.6 (do)	M34

Vivian Wheatland Lieut Col
Cmdg 258th Brigade R.F.A.

51st Divisional Artillery.

258th BRIGADE

ROYAL FIELD ARTILLERY

AUGUST 1 9 1 6 :::::::

WAR DIARY
or
INTELLIGENCE SUMMARY

(Erase heading not required.)

Place	Date	Hour	Summary of Events and Information	Remarks and references to Appendices
In the field	1/8/16		Brigade in action in CATERPILLAR WOOD slightly shelled by enemy during day. 2 men wounded	WD34
	2/8/16		Brigade in action. Positions heavily shelled by enemy.	WD34
	3/8/16		Brigade in action. Positions very heavily shelled by enemy. LIEUT I. GALLETLY KILLED IN ACTION. LIEUT-COL. P.C.MACFARLANE WOUNDED (SHOCK,SHELL & GAS). 2/LIEUT F.B. SANDERSON WOUNDED. LIEUT & ADJT R. WILSON WOUNDED SLIGHT (AT DUTY). 8 other ranks wounded.	WD34
	4/8/16		Brigade in action. (first day casualties) Att slight enemy shelling. 2/LIEUT G.R. ANDERSON to hospital sick. 1 other rank wounded.	WD34
	5/8/16		Brigade in action. Quiet day.	WD34
	6/8/16		Brigade in action. Shelled by enemy. 3 other ranks wounded	WD34
	7/8/16		Brigade in action. 2/Lieut A. GUTHRIE slightly wounded (at duty) 1 man killed in action.	WD34
	8/8/16		Brigade in action. 1 man killed of wounds received during day. 4 other ranks wounded. LIEUT-COL P.C. MACFARLANE to ENGLAND per hospital ship.	WD34
	9/8/16		Relief of Bde. by sections commenced. First sections of 17th DA. relieve 1 section per Battery. Sections relieved move to WAGON LINES at BECORDEL.	WD34
	10/8/16		Relief of Bde by 17th D.A. completed. Bde in Wagon Lines at BECORDEL. 2/LIEUT F.B. SANDERSON reported DIED OF WOUNDS received on 3/8/16.	WD34
	11/8/16		Brigade moves to BONNAY.	WD34
	12/8/16		at BONNAY. Captain J.B. MILNE A/255 posted to A/258. 2/Lieuts D. NICOLL and J.M. FARLIE from 256th Bde posted to C/258.	WD34
	13/8/16		Brigade in BONNAY. A.B Batteries move to entrain.	WD34
	14/8/16		C Battery and Hqrs move to entrain. A.B.& C Batteries entrain at LONGUEAU. Hqrs entrains at SALEUX. A.B.& C Batteries detrain at STEENBECQUE and THIENNES and move to SERCUS. LIEUT-COL F.T. OLDHAM from 7th Bde R.F.A. posted to Bde. 2/Lieut J.E. TODD to hospital sick. Advance party of officers per in advance of relief to N.Z. Artillery at ARMENTIERES.	WD34
	15/8/16		Bde Hqrs detrains at ARQUES and moves to SERCUS. Bde now in SERCUS. One officer per battery joins advance party at ARMENTIERES.	WD34

WAR DIARY or INTELLIGENCE SUMMARY

(Erase heading not required.)

Place	Date	Hour	Summary of Events and Information	Remarks and references to Appendices
In the field	16/8/16	—	Commencement of relief of NZFA. Hqrs and 1 section Aus battery move from SERCUS to ARMENTIERES.	M734
	17/8/16		Sections in action require, Completion of relief. Remaining sections move to positions at ARMENTIERES. Hqrs of Bde takes over from 4th NZFA Bde at 10.30PM on completion of relief.	M734
	18/8/16		Batteries in action. Registration.	M734
	19/8/16		Batteries in action. Registration.	M734
	20/8/16		Batteries in action. Registration.	M734
	21/8/16		Batteries in action. Registration. 51st (H) D.A. Operation Order No 46. 258th Bde R.F.A. to be broken up in re-organisation of Divisional Artillery. A/258 to 255th Bde. B/258 to 256th Bde. C/258. ½ to 255th Bde and ½ to 256th Bde.	M734
	22/8/16		Re-organisation being completed.	M734

J. J. Ottorum
Lieut Colonel
Commanding 258th Bde R.F.A.

www.ingramcontent.com/pod-product-compliance
Lightning Source LLC
Chambersburg PA
CBHW081458160426
43193CB00013B/2525